flipped eye publishing

Werewolf of London

simple words, rendered sublime

Werewolf of London

flipped eye publishing
www.flippedeye.net

First published by flipped eye publishing © 2021
Copyright © 2021, Niall O'Sullivan

Cover Concept & Finishing © flipped eye publishing, 2017, 2021
Cover Letter Typeface Design & Front Layout © D237, 2017 | www.d237.com

This book is typeset in Book Antiqua and Palatino from Linotype GmbH.

Earlier versions of poems in this book have appeared in *Rising, South Bank Poetry, The Dream of the Fisherman's Wife, New Boots and Pantisocracies The Morning Star* and *Londonist*.

ISBN-13: 978-1-905233-62-5

Supported using public funding by

ARTS COUNCIL ENGLAND

LOTTERY FUNDED

for my daughters

Werewolf of London

Werewolf of London

Contents

New(ish)

Now is Not the Time for Politics

Werewolf of London

Old(ish)

New(ish)

Ikiru

The commuters thrashing
their hatchbacks up Dog
Kennel Hill cannot see my
daughter, pressed tight to
my chest, they can only
make out my trilby-
sporting silhouette,
perched on a swing in the
empty playground, not
unlike that beleaguered
Tokyo civil servant,
mumbling a sentimental
dirge to himself as the
tumour that has feasted
on his generous spirit is
almost ready for the bill.

. . . inochi mijikashi
koi seyo otome
kurokami no iro
asenu ma ni . . .

From where I am, this
bright Autumn morning
could almost be a Spring
day. My baby girl laughs
at the sky as we teeter
towards it. Life is short.

Happy Hour In Herne Hill

Which way
did you come from,
following dream paths at night,
while snow is still deep
in this mountain recess?
-Ryokan

"No, I don't think community is about talking to someone in the shop. When I
choose to have my community experience, I want to choose where to have it - at
the youth centre or the mosque or wherever." -Baroness Warsi, Minister for
Communities, December 2013

Two figures cruise through afternoon fog,
hoods up, backs arched, heads upright and alert,
toes nudging BMX pedals a quarter click,
tyres turning the pace of a pit bull sneaking up
on a squirrel for the tenth time,
ears tuned for the treble of hoity toity chatter
of spoilt arrivistes that still go to school.

The Herne Hill Forum will soon fizzle with mild alert.
Tell your kids to come straight home, iPhones pocketed,
to seasonal ragu, to the Au Pair's humility,
where the mortgage is paid and the forsythia's in bloom.

Oh what a ripple they will send, these BMX lads
with their hand-me-down sportswear and their balls half-dropped,
snatching phones from gloved hands then raring off,
caning the pedals as Phoebe whinnies through the speaker
about plans to plonk a Tesco by the Sainsbury's Local
while Brixton, yes Brixton, gets a Waitrose!

They are boys that never knew the guiding hand of a father
They are image library avatars for broken Britain
They are victims failed by the education system
They are toerags in need of a fucking slap

They are taking the cha-cha-cha out of chav
They are almost invisible and so they shall remain

I spotted the pair of them as I left Sunray Gardens,
where a swan set down for a few moments on the pond
before the seagulls sent him packing over brown-roofs.
While I knew their game, I didn't pocket my phone;
I clasped it so the ridges of my broken metacarpals
would whiten with the will to swipe the bumfluff from their chins.
With my trilby and long coat I could be a Hitchcock villain
if I wasn't pushing Daughter in a newly-bought Maclaren.

Minutes later, I clip heels with swivel wheels, a curmudgeon before my
        time,
grumbling "fucking toffs" as I swerve through a three-fold queue for a
        fee-paying CofE primary school production
about a pair of penniless asylum seekers on a donkey (the unborn child
        is not the husband's),
distracting superstitious shepherds, fleecing frankincense from faddish
        astrologers,
exhausting the patience of beleaguered hoteliers before disturbing the
        peace of their livestock.

For now the only money lenders are a couple of miles up the Walworth
        Road and the only market's the farmer's market, every
        Sunday,
on the newly pedestrianised parade:
        organic produce
        soft cheeses
        ceramics
        preserves
        falafel...

Put on your best Barbour jacket, come down, bask in the sense of
        community,
unless you're viewing through the smeared glass of the launderette
        window,
then the message seems to be, "Piss off, your kind aren't needed any
        more.
Piss off to the suburbs, to the Thames estuary, to where the affordable
        housing is almost so,
where your kiddies are guaranteed a place in an Ofsted baiting primary
        school,
where the local superstore stocks:
        tents
        televisions
        every size and variety of cereal
        (but no okra)
to where you might just spot a strayed seal between widening banks,
        just don't hold your breath for a bus.
Piss off, piss off, the pub's large sports screen has been replaced by a
        mirror and this cream cheese and parsley crêpe is not for you."

Things have changed so quickly round here, even the creatives are
        feeling the pinch:
they who colonised railway arches and empty shops, lit up our cultural
        dark ages with their MacBook screens,
transubstantiating old and used into vintage and retro.
Angelheaded hipsters, searching for the free WiFi connection to the
        starry dynamos in the cloud servers of night,
their dreams too big for the cul-de-sacs they grew up in, finding their
        voice under the shadow of tower blocks,
seeking bohemia, Albion in Londinium, to be among their own, away
        from "normal people".
But now is the hour of the leasehold harvest and the cadavers behind

glass displays
are not so much Bacon, Hirst or Goya as they are free range, organic and
        locally reared.

They are the latest exhibitors in the Salon des Refusés
They have never done a proper day's work in their lives
They are the plague rats of gentrification
They are misunderstood, wilfully so
They are cutting edge, asymmetrically so
They are gratefully acknowledging the assistance of the Arts Council England
When they speak of community, it isn't ironic

Still, in the station subway, just up from the garden ornament shop
        that's replaced the barber I will never miss,
where pigeons still find roosting space among the mounted spikes and
        anti-climb paint,
some community-minded spirit has parked an upright piano against
        crumbling brickwork
and what would seem another Foxton's sponsored trojan horse is quite
        the opposite
as a skittish youth unplugs white headphones, cracks his knuckles to
        practice Brahms.
The creaking, dripping, shit-smeared arches attain an undertone of
        sentience
and his soul seems as old as quiver-scrawled notes from the hand of the
        master himself.
Toff, chav, alkie, copper, rasta, junky, yummy mummy, gap-yah
        student, hipster, imam, spinster—
all these appearances seem like pound store wrapping when music
        speaks through them.

But hunched over the keys today, an old Jamaican gentleman plays one-

handed,
his other hand outstretched as he hits all the wrong notes in all the right
    places,
If ya buy me a drink I'll play you a tune... A two-handed tune, a tempting
    offer...

There's just an alleyway's difference between the gastropubs, boutiques,
    delicatessens
and the roti restaurant, Afro barbers, money transfer internet cafe
—a little Brixtonian, Windrush ripple you'll struggle to find in some
    parts of Brixton these days—
where you might spot the great dub poet himself, puffing on a rolly
    outside the bookies.
Who knows how the piano man keeps a roof over his head when
    playing blues for booze?
Maybe bought outright through a local co-op when the banks refused
    loans to *his kind*;
or got himself a council place when the old working classes made their
    exodus to the suburbs;
ah, the council flats, still standing when the middle-income earners have
    been squeezed out;
the tenants hanging on, when the creatives have sought another slum to
    terraform;
hanging on until it's time for regeneration, when it's time to outsource
    the poverty.

He is a smoky function room of dancehall tunes half-remembered through
    fumbling fingers
He is pissing away what's left of his days, but doing it in style
He remembers the riots but he was at home when they happened, officer
He was the change in his own time, the change that is now being swept up
He is a copy-written blurb about the area's cultural history and authenticity

You could say it's been all change here since the Effra was banished to
        intestinal Victorian vaults—
the currents that once ferried Elizabeth's barge towards the bent knee
        of Walter now commute our bobbing Richards to assured
        oblivion.
They trickled on, unobserved, when the two-foot water main burst last
        summer, making a docile lake of the bustling junction
and a write-off of the private dentists, electric store and the Half Moon
        pub;
rescue workers in kayaks played the role of waterfowl, as, above
        flooded restaurants and shopfronts,
first floor tenants woke to stare blearily through windows at the water's
        lip lapping a lazy arm's depth from their sills
whilst, two floors down, basements lived up to their metaphorical
        clichés, documents swirling free of their paperclip moorings.

When I first moved here more than a decade ago, I was also partially
        developed,
a twenty-something blow-hard with shovel-calloused palms,
a class apart from the embryonic professionals drifting in from North of
        the river.
I walked with wide, frenzied strides, the chip on my shoulder not as
        smooth and sanded as it is today.
How did I get here? Where am I going? The playgroup, the
        supermarket, a few hundred days more, then the suburbs?

I am pushing forty while pushing a buggy
I am as out of place as my 90s playlist
I am forgetting, once again, to stock up on nappies
I am a soft-palmed man of letters dry humping the dead wood of my credible,
        blue collar past

We are hanging on. As light fittings rust and and rents exponentiate.
    The three of us.
We do not belong here, but it's a nice place not to belong to.
We are too vulgar perhaps to see our marching orders writ large on
    Estate Agent placards.
When the air clears and the first spring buds erupt, we'll only exist in
    pixelated Street View screenshots
because it wasn't these stacked bricks and gravel drives that we
    belonged to, no, we always belonged to the fog.

route 68 walworth road

the mind itself is a rowdy top deck
so I have no problem dipping into Walcott
despite the ruckus down back
kids giggling   build up   scream crescendo
causing mum to clutch a flip phone to her chest

> *shut up ya noise*

our eyes will us outside
to pluck ripeness from fruit and veg vistas
to be by the small booth

> *international phone cards*
> *watch straps*

next to the crouching seller, to know

> *eek a nomics*

what's busting from his speakers
causing the odd rocking jaw clenching
rolling on, past the 24 hour bagel shop

> *so much time so few bagels*

past the flapping banner of
the WORLDWIDE POWER CHURCH MINISTRIES OF JESUS

> *the Lord is my accountant,*
> *I shall not declare*

past the curiously named MIXED BLESSINGS BAKERY

> *strong hands don't do irony*

irish bars steadfast as failure
dark doors swallowing the bookies' flotsam

> *whack fol de daddy-o*

past the last occupied flats of the Heygate

> *we're improving your area*
> *we need you to leave*

my eyes return to terza rima

sea almonds . . .
bougainvillea . . .

the littlest one screams again
and then the slap

Godfrey's Yard

When that old maroon Ford Capri limped into Godfrey's yard,
he couldn't believe it, the same damn rude boy ride
with a new exhaust to replace the one he'd drilled holes in
back in the day, when it was Bodie and Doyle's chariot of choice
loud and sleek, just like he was, a slim nasty body
chasing girls and bucks with barely twenty-five years on the clock,
and now, thirty later, he wants to get in, drum his fingertips
on the wheel to the rhythm of the engine, hah!

Bass boxes were only needed after cars got quiet.

Just one more time to run his palm along
the craters made in the back seat by all the sizes and tones
of booty that he rode to glory; the hot rock burns
pocking the upholstery due to the weed shortage of '79.

But he doesn't. He strolls out, plucks his keys, *bleep-bleep*:
a silver Audi ready for the drive back to Surrey.

Two hours later, the only living thing left in the yard
is Saul, the latest in a long pedigree of Lambeth Rottweiler.
He's the lone soldier defending a graveyard of kings
against intruders, pigeons, those uncatchable rats;

if he doesn't get a bite now, the day shift will do...

He sniffs and pads away the itchy hours
until the car horn of a Shih Tzu's heat blows
in from the local green and hits him bang on,
stock still, stiff in more ways than one, a satellite for scent,
chemistry of intent running through a perfect machine,

circuitry between balls and brain in perfect tandem—
then a cold breeze full of monoxide and railing rust
knocks it out of him, his snout returns to the ground

and sniffs yesterday's turds. They're still his.

The Dog

"The postman will just leave it on the doorstep and then it'll get taken by a dog." Mrs O'Sullivan on why I should stay home in the morning in case the postman knocks.

And so it is, as the decline in our national postal service
drops another notch towards its knockdown privatisation,
the slightly stoned delivery man forgets the "we missed you" slip,
dumps your copy of *English as a Lingua Franca, third edition*
and grinds his van's gearbox through waking Lambeth streets.
All odds would be on one of the local bagheads
or skiving toerags filching it, until
the dog appears: more chimaera than mongrel,
part pitbull, part mastiff, part urban fox,
one red eye, one blue—a glare that halts
all those that move to pet it.
He clamps your package in his fetid chops
and skulks downhill, past four bores
that make the same gag to long-suffering partners
about how the Post Office will employ anyone these days.
On he trots, past newly-sprouted coffee bars
and posh-a-brac boutiques,
through a rusting flap of sheet metal
that shuts off a once busy alley, now tendrilled
with strings of glistening blackberries,
threaded with glass shards and used prophylactics.
From there he schleps fifty yards of railway until
he reaches the overgrown entrance of an engine room,
its whereabouts and utility forgotten, spits your
precious package onto a steaming heap,
the hundreds that never made it over at least ten years,
damp and drool heavy, new homes for snails.
He surveys his horde with some canine equivalent of satisfaction
then drops onto his belly to grind his teeth on the femur
of the last schmuck to follow him this far
to his cosy den of bones and unread words.

interglacial

25°C straw hat & sun cream makes me feel like I'm on holiday. daughter gets the factor 50 despite her filipino dna. when the ice sheet barred the path north of what is now condemned to be watford, human footfall patterned the turf of doggerland, mutations filtered through. dry pallid skin to nab vitamin d from dimming doses of sun. the welsh geneticist steve jones said that if a cro-magnon sat next to you on a train you'd probably change seats; if a neanderthal sat next to you on a train you'd move to another train. if a romanian sat next to nigel farage on a train then the romanian would have grounds to feel uncomfortable. they dredged up hippo bones from the banks of the thames. the romans, the normans, jimi hendrix & that lone doomed whale were all drawn to take part in this riverside sprawl. my parents came from ireland with £17 between them. if you voted UKIP last may you need to stay out of my life.

The Beautiful Sarth

It's just after eleven and each soul
on the Victoria line reads from their phones
or thumbs their way onto the next level

of Angry Birds, when suddenly some loon
begins to shout before the doors slide shut
at some young man who's just got off the train,

"That's right, you better get off, immigrant!
Go play them bloody drums in Africa!"
We stay silent, there's not even a tut,

until a black guy opposite me mutters
"He's obviously a good friend of John Terry..."
And, after stifled giggles, I rejoinder:

"There's drums in Europe too, apparently"
And like that final scene in Spartacus
when all those faithful men stand up to cry

that it is their name too, other commuters
state other places where they play the drums
—like Scotland, South Korea and Croatia—

and after each location named there comes
a louder round of chuckles til the man
that made the racist comment sits and squirms—

and after drum location number ten,
he sullenly whispers "I've calmed down now."
His stop arrives. Her shuffles off and then

the man across from me grins and bellows
in a voice that echoes through the platform's rafters,
"Be careful mate, there's drums in Pimlico!"

and the train carries off our ridicule and laughter.

ordinary people

poetry should engage with ordinary people. who sit in their gardens and watch butterflies flit about the buddleia. who drive moderate distances through rapeseed fields to places they feel obligated to be. who go out once every decade or so to watch their third favourite music act and come home sober and disappointed. who buy seven jazz albums before realising they don't like jazz. who married for love, who married for fear. who move their sex toys from the sock drawer to a box in the attic and almost forget about them. who remember to erase their browser history. who hate their job but love their children. who hate their children but love their job. whose lives twine with the lives of others around telephone poles and not much else. who find momentary happiness in a first glug of beer at a pub bench just off a motorway before despising every moment of the holiday. oh, I would write for them if I could. who doesn't want a piece of whsmith and the O_2 arena? ordinary people, where would they be without us?

England

I'm willing to get to know you. maybe I didn't have time to before. I was a bloody irish whelp when my cord was cut. england was a can of coca cola bought from the offy and shared with my brother after mass. it was half-cooked fish fingers for lunch & nuns in the classroom. it was the bmx ramp in the triangular green on the estate when I ran over an old man's foot & he said nothing. it was the daily mail when it was all hate and no sidebar. I learned to love maggie & hate the argies. I first knew you as a football team that sang a song. I properly loved you for a while when I left the flat industrial shithole & studied in bath. hills and sandstone blew my mind. london claimed me after that. it was the gallery's fault. I climbed into a rothko painting and never found my way back out. you became that green stuff that whizzed by the window on the train to liverpool. you were a pub called the black boy. I want us to have another chance, england. I thought you were a cup of weak tea & a picture of the queen. you might be red ochre on a cave wall. you might be inconsolable weeping in a service station at 4am. england, I have turned more of your soil between my politically correct palms than any of your suited propagandists.

On finding two toilets within a single cubicle at Canary Wharf

While most of the country is left without a pot to piss in, here I am with
    two.
Under a plated glass prick full of little prick homunculi, I too find
    abundance.
I am internally ip-dipping as to which one I shall anoint in the same
    way that I hovered between Labour and Green on polling day.
Does this arrangement help bankers to high five and cross streams after
    another day of "smashing it"?
Or is this designed for a tender moment between father and son, *Look at
    me, I am old but I'm happy...*
Perhaps this stands as the ultimate definition of trickle-down
    economics?
Oh what art school anarchy it would be to piss on the tiles between, if
    it weren't for the image of a stoical attendant with a curved
    spine and hourly quotas to hit.
I poise above the ballot, allow the illusion of free will to take hold and
    veer to the left.

Change the World One County at a Time, Start with Essex

We catch the early train from Liverpool Street
and meet the sun halfway, its first rays making bunny shadows
across long Essex fields using real bunnies—
before the rusting sprawl of Harwich International
makes a nonsense of the buzzword "post-industrial":
creaking schooners, packed crates, splintered pallets,
worldly goods, Tesco-bound, from China with Love. . .
we reach our destination, Dovercourt,
a puddle of piss gleams coldly in the entrance hall.
This is where they filmed the Brit-com Hi-De-Hi,
the very site where Peggy harboured Yellowcoat dreams
is now a housing estate, flapping George Crosses and Sky dishes,
our first line of defence should the Vikings ever return.

In the function room of a star-shedding hotel
where corks have been popped and noses broken,
we convene—a gaggle of thesps, poets, musicians
painters and potters, not referred to as artists but

creatives.
Sandwiches droop on doyleys, stale bourbon crèmes betray
the many miles to the nearest Arabica bean.
The workshop co-ordinator has no need for caffeine,
he's buzzing on the tartrazine of the mission statement,
for even failed actors need something to believe in:
"Today's education system is out of date,
tailored towards the needs of the industrial revolution. . .
What's needed is cre-a-tiv-i-ty, to reflect
the 'post-industrial' society we now live in. . .
and so, with all this in mind,
does anyone have any questions regarding creativity?"
I raise my hand— "Van Gogh could have been a carpenter,

Sylvia Plath a PA: is creativity always a good thing?"
I'm later told by another creative, that lifting an arse cheek
and farting out loud would have gone down better.

Lunch arrives, business cards flutter from palm to palm.
I step out, cross the road, plod onto the beach front.
A gentle drizzle rolls in as I buy an ice cream
and eat it in full view of some unemployed locals
then lob stones into the churning grey swell,
that ultimate engine of creativity where
this carbon-based shambles got started.

Love Song of a Lapsed Materialist

Homebound, on a District Line carriage,
I shoulder your head to stop the world, press
my cheek to the top of your crown and hear
something, throbbing, knocking from within.

It could be the echo of your heart, hammering
iron through your veins; or the soft, wet brain
beneath your ink black hair and dull white skull;
and permeating through your every cell—

the judder of rails, the humming wires.
And I'm reminded of that Zen koan:
the runaway couple who returned home
after exile sweetened childhood memories.

Expecting the worst of a wronged father's wrath,
the man advised his wife to wait outside
and crossed the threshold only to meet
the bemused father's incredulity.

"She's been ill in her room these past two years!"
and at that point both versions of her appeared –
one from outside, one from the bedroom door –
and, like two matte layers, both were merged together.

But as I meet this version of you revealed
by the physicalist census of your parts –
and the *you* revealed by what the word *love* fails –
my heart pumps blood to my brain and my mind

tries to picture my heart. And though words spark
from the shock of their collision –
for all those times I swore they were the same –
I cannot clasp these two *yous* together.

Gordale Scar

after James Ward (1815)

It is not true that the gaze travels outwards,
over the heraldic beasts, between the limestone
hulks, skimming the stream where the last
surviving glints of light twinkle, onward
into the numb dark where minds are not welcome.

It is the scar itself and John Bull's eye
that funnel into you, breach the iris,
pummel the retina, flume through the optic nerve
to ambush the cortex, seize synapses to find —
the flags packed up, the fortress long deserted.

A 1956 edition of Moby Dick recalls its many years at Clapham Library

I am the greatest book you've never read—
not Ulysses, these pages don't descend
into a verbose Dublin underworld—
I am instead a rocky, churning trawl,
a journey of the fragile human soul
into the soulless fathoms, not that all
that hefted my few hundred pages home
completed the journey. Close me tight
and view the bookmarked stack of my pages;
the sediments of well-thumbed early chapters
becoming clearer with the slow descent
into the quadrants few ventured into.
The insert glued into my inside cover
is barnacled with criss-crossing due dates
a logbook of the many disparate souls,
who journeyed with the hammock-stacked players—
most climbed in bed with Queequeg, never woke;
while others dozed off during the sermon
on Jonah in the creaking, salt-flecked church;
while others set off from New Haven's shores
to run adrift on Melville's derivations:
taxonomies on harpoons, spermaceti
and questionable natural histories.
Others made it to the crashing end,
the whole boat, with it's crew and madnesses,
the white whale and its wider, whiter wake,
folded into the ocean's eyeless depths
before my covers too must be shut tight.

Mark this one date, January '57,
the first to read through every single page

was but a boy of fourteen awkward years.
He'd never seen the ocean's blue for real
but instead held my sturdy hardback spine
above a steaming tub of piped water
drawn for tuppence down the Clapham Baths.
On reading of the moment Pip went under —
to sink towards the ocean's amnesiac bed,
to lose his mind the moment that he glimpsed
the void or, possibly, the mind of God,
or maybe both — the reader placed me down
and dunked his head under the bath water
to glimpse his own body through the blur;
seeming more alien in its becoming,
not quite the waving weeds and nibbling mouths
but not far off in its increasing strangeness.

This next date, October '87 —
I was read during countless commutes
across the Vauxhall Bridge then Underground;
then eight hours spent behind a bank counter
where wealth slipped through her nimble fingers all day;
before the slog back home where her mother
had sprung the kids from school and filled their bellies.
Her journey — crammed upstairs on the Routemaster
and rattling, cough-wracked smoking carriages —
was the only escape that she could manage.
How strange, perhaps, to shun the morning paper
for an all male crew where the non-whites
were casually described as "savages",
though at the same time seen more as equals,
appreciated for their foam-hewn skills
than softly-spoken managers treated her;
nor customers that waited in the queue

for positions other than hers to open up.
She wondered if the pull of this voyage
was part of some pre-lingual memory
of when she came across on the Windrush,
within her mother's belly, breathing water.

This final date, September '11,
was stamped for a young man who learned the lesson
that gangs won't look for you in libraries.
The bookishness he carried from childhood
kept him from the tug of peer pressure,
kept him from going out that night
when London burned. He locked his bedroom door
and read of Ahab, roped to his obsession.
As bricks found shop displays, and clipper flames
became hell dioramas, he read the words,
"Towards thee I roll, thou all-destroying
but unconquering whale; to the last
I grapple with thee, from hell's heart I stab at thee;
for hate's sake I spit my last breath at thee."
...and by the time my due date came around,
the boys that he grew up with had set off
on lengthy sentences, Crown's messages
to any other lost, street corner crews,
drawn from small worlds into greater madness.

That was the moment when I was retired,
to leave the telling of this epic trawl
to plastic-cocooned paperback editions.
Deemed too dogeared for the antique market,
they scribbled 50p in my top corner
and beached me loosely on the quick sale counter.
Then, a familiar grip raises me up,

as if the Pequod's shell has finally
been dredged up from its unmarked resting place.
A slight tremble of age or recognition
ripples through my caved-in, taped-up spine.
As his failing focus marks the date,
January '57, he remembers
that some of these finger smudges are his own.
A fresh wind fills his soul's exhausted sails.
An *I* within a wide expanse. Ismeal.

A Perfect Record

We arrive at the same time as he does
to some stirring mid-nineties anthem.
The arena's almost empty, we've got hours

until the main event, the young and handsome
prospect enters next to wild applause
from twenty family members. Then the customs

of referee's instruction and touched gloves.
The bell rings and the prospect goes in fast,
the journeyman covers, ducks and weaves—

they always rush right in, their flailing fists
are keen to make short work of him, he knows
from all these monthly pocket money fights

fed to the debut boys, his return blows
are known to not cause problems, his efforts
revolve around giving the punters a show

while not taking too many heavy shots
so he can make his losers' split next time
to pay the bills and keep the missus sweet.

She's at home watching X Factor, the chime
of the last bell provides longed for relief,
he hugs the prospect, whispers lies to him

about how he'll have a successful life
and not be a domestic nearly ran.
His string of losses holds back debt and grief—

a rosary necklace of bearable pains
that gives a chance to those he loves the most.
He's gone before the knucklehead refrains

of *smash his 'ead 'in!* ring from post to post,
the slobs in suits, the patriotic orgies
of jingoistic bias and lewd boasts

at ring girls with their labial wedgies.
But all these rituals are yet to come,
we once again scan through the programme's pages.

The journeyman begins his journey home.

Now is Not the
Time for Politics

I

The speck of life that stirs within your womb
is now a fact sanctioned by our GP.
A place within the crowded Polis looms

and so begins the trend to entropy
from nature's realm to citizen of state,
from breath to name before the first nappy

is, like our blessed leaders, full of shit.
And yet, it's never felt so radical—
the spawning sport that's played from whale to gnat,

how the mundane becomes so magical.
I guess all reveries become statistics
as poems become periodicals—

ephemeral pleasures. Considered. Listed.

II

Week nine, now you're the size of a grape;
all organs present and you've lost your tail,
seven months until you make the leap

from viewless womb into the teary vale.
I'm at the blues bar, early for the stag,
I'm Nially No Mates, solitary male,

adrift from the reverie of the pack.
I down my Murphy's, fire off a few tweets,
outside the sun blazes, inside time drags,

the boys are running thirty minutes late.
I'm counting beats to Howling Wolf's *Evil*,
you mark the 4-4 of your mother's heart.

The both of us, snug in our darkened bubbles.

III

Labour hasn't started, so we snatch
whatever sleep we can as hours stream
like fluids through a drip. I keep a watch

for midwives that appear like fleeting dreams
and vanish with the words "I'll go find out..."
the curtains flutter, they never return.

Before I left at 4am last night,
I heard a newborn's first cries down the hall.
Despite the rain that sputtered down outside,

the birds on every branch sang loud and shrill.
Right now, a blue partition cuts us off
from the Polish single-mum-to-be's sad call

for doctors, birthing room and pain relief.
And you, my love, are somehow able to,
curl up against the chaos and drift off.

I self-administer an espresso.

IV

Okay, daughter dearest, hear this right,
that crazy stuff each side of you is noise.
That crazy stuff in front of you is light.

The warbling beyond our curtain is
some Pentecostals giving Satan the boot
from a bed provided by the NHS.

The NHS aren't devils or devout,
they are the country's socialist backbone,
the young nurses that once cried "Maggie out!"

are still walking the wards where you were born,
though the moral high ground that they tread
might soon be privatised by George Osborne

before that hated, heckled Baroness
has sunk into her private trust pillows
to die a premium, elitist death.

Oh dear, I'm talking politics, I know,
it's yet to stain the mind of your sweet ilk,
but since we're skin to skin I must disclose

like Thatcher, my man boobs won't give milk.

V

I take the trek up just one flight of stairs,
scrub my hands and arms and walk on through
to find you strung with drip lines and thick wires.

Your readings have been good, steady but slow.
You're doing your bit, under watchful eye
of surrogate aunties—Filipinos

and Irish nurses too. You sleep as I
take you into my arms and whisper how
your mother's getting strong as well. Your cries

are easily sated, though my own
still bubble upwards, lava like, sudden—
and though you tip the scales at seven pounds,

your humble heft helps me to hold it down,
maintain composure, keep the long sob in.
Your short vowels hold back pity's pale poison,

the sweet song of the smallest violin.

VI

Outside the double-glazed window, just across
from where my baby girl snoozes away,
pumped full of milk and gripping my fingers,

the Power Station almost fades to grey,
within the week-long, secular deluge.
I forget what it's like to walk in rain—

the seven days we've spent under this roof.

VII

The hospital gives me the chance to bring
the First Noble Truth into focus,
for all that breathe are also suffering,

but when I head outside to catch the bus,
within the clammy streets of Camberwell,
it's not long til I ditch the mindfulness

and tell a stranger to go fuck themselves.

VIII

...and just like that, we're back. The hospital
is once again the house upon the hill
and we are but a quaint suburban couple

toting their newborn, fat-cheeked baby girl,
so unremarkable, nothing of note.
We take our sleeps in tiny shots between meals.

We pull the blinds down, flutter out a vote.

IX

I try to picture this child in my arms
as an old woman in a distant time
in spite of climate change or nuclear bombs.

I wonder if she'll read these dodgy rhymes
to great-great-grandchildren I'll never know?
Well, are you currently reading these lines?

Have I been gone a long, long time?
                                        Hello

Werewolf of London

The Argument

But remember this Dr Glendun, the werewolf instinctively seeks to kill the thing it loves best.
-Dr Yogami (Werewolf of London, 1935)

On conquering the heights of that stark peak,
gaze trained for the mariphasia flower
that only blooms during moonlit hours,
I was attacked by some carpet-faced freak.
Throughout the hours before the fever broke,
I wondered if, back home, you dreamt of lovers,
old flames with supernormal carnal powers:
in their stark heat had your resolve proved weak?
It wasn't the pallid moon that caused the change
but that old flame whose name slipped from your tongue
the last time we reciprocated lust.
And now blood trickles down the city's drains,
your petals bloomed before my fangs have sprung:
the beast seeks to destroy what it loves most.

The Laboratory

The flower's yet to bloom, its white petals
clenched tight within hard, brown bud.
I reposition the moon lamp, bark instructions
to my assistant (in matters such as this
I only trust myself and idiot lackeys
who can only confess to fat, stupid wives
and fellow inebriates down the ale house).
Beyond the bolted steel door, wisdom festers
within leather-bound jackets on polished shelves
and in the gardens outside, the pitchers,
flytraps and lobster pots spread their green limbs
while digesting their scuttling prey.
An automobile engine cuts out on the gravel drive.
The howling of wolves from the Regents Park Zoo
echoes through the grand vestibule
where the deep red carpet rides the curve of the stairs
to the perfumed unease of the bedroom.

Metamorphosis

The transformation is no cross-fade paralysis
nor bone-crunching, flesh-ripping frenzy,
it is no different within to the last choice you made
though you always knew which way it would go
and the choice was nothing more than pantomime,
a necessary ritual, the having it out with oneself
was really a masonic handshake,
a changing of the guard to let one self fade
as the other steps forward to take the wheel;
for the stuck-up botanist, a clumped knot
of convention and regret to give way
to the widow's peak and a slight
pronouncement of fingernail and fang,
the tux still fits and the caps still gleam.

The wolf does not wake, snarling within
a trashed basement, his evening suit shredded,
no, he calmly slips on his coat and cap,
crunches the lab door shut, treads lightly.

The Testimony of Mrs Moncaster

"They're always high and mighty,
Well-bred and long-wordy,
the ones that pay up a week in advance—
but you don't know the real man
'til you've took a nip of gin
and seen him framed by the keyhole.

"And I thought I'd seen it all,
the bank manager's hairy arse
up and down on Boozy Beryl;
the Superintendent dolled up
as the Princess of Wales. . .

"But when I heard howling
from the garret upstairs
and crouched down to
grab me an eyeful. . .

"The whole bloody bottle
went and slipped from me grip,
me poor giddy heart
never had such a shock
since me wedding night. . ."

The End

When the dying wolfman began to speak,
to thank the Chief of Police for the bullet,
to apologise to his wife and wish her happiness,
then to breathe his last, upside down on the stairs—
it was already familiar to her,
she'd seen that expression, the gaping mouth,
that carnivore glare in the last thrusting minute
each time he shot his useless seed in her
and how the next thing he said was always, "Sorry. . ."

And now her childhood sweetheart is flying her to America,
she watches the gleaming ripples of the sea below,
feels the engine's power throughout the trembling cockpit.
Her thoughts seem so weightless but she knows
that soon she'll get to see the other side, for wolves
don't ooze charm in drawing rooms, they do not guide you
hand in hand, up the stairs. . . the wolf appears
in the bedroom as if he has climbed through
the window and slipped into the lover's skin
only this time, she's also going to crouch on all fours,
bare her shining white teeth and howl.

Old(ish)

Confession

Father Rourke took my first confession.
His voice was solemn, ravaged and unmistakable
on the other side of our shared dark.

I sent my sins over to him,
once emptied, I refilled with Our Fathers and Hail Marys
and returned to the big green world to sin again.

During Sunday services he'd grumble through
the Gospels, waking us halfway
with a plague of coughs and splutters.

With the crisp white sleeve of his vestments,
he'd wipe his phlegm from the Bible,
then from his clean shaved face.

The adults gave each other knowing looks
and whispered in the paddy club about
his fondness for the scotch and fags,

but I knew it was more: those petty sins
we suburbanites poured into him
each month's third Saturday

had formed a black tar inside his belly,
if not a tar then a kind of worm,
killing him from the inside.

I had long left the town when I heard
that the cancer had had its way.
I didn't attend the funeral.

The whole parish turned up

through partial guilt at having killed him,
they wept clean tears, lowered the coffin,

made sure the lid was shut tight,
that the ground was patted down hard,
genuflected three times

went with their little new-born sins
and the big ugly ones they never confessed,
back to the silent houses of that shitty town.

buddleia

many faced and silent
the orient has dawned upon the city
the breeze is thick with seed
life digs into dirt
prods into grime
finds a way

do not assume
that this lone branch
sprung from brick
feels loneliness
not with its progeny
sentried along railways
their purple flames emerging
from redundant chimneys

we can howl
and shout
from smashed out windows
as loud
and drunk as we like

our words will never mint the dark
or say so precisely
what we so simply are
to places
people

we will never know

The Limit

300ft above the Hanger Lane gyratory
a police helicopter breaches the cusp of its jurisdiction
and sweeps from the sunset to the dusk
towards the crowded towers of the South Acton Estate.
The engine's growl seeps into the bedroom
of my brother's Acton flat,
I hate that sound, he says to me
as he changes baby Ossian,
makes it feel like a police state.
I tell him about a police chase show
I saw on TV, how those choppers are kitted out
with infrared heat-seeking cameras
if one ever hooks onto you
the best thing to do is too keep running,
jump garden fences, kick guard dogs in the face,
ignore the shreds that rose bushes rip from your skin,
use one way systems to your advantage
make that high risk sprint across the motorway,
keep zigzagging 'til that chopper runs out of fuel.
Only then is it safe to hide and form your strategy.
Still, you could never escape that low hum
and the message it broadcasts into every living room.
which means nothing to baby Ossian,
four weeks on this earth and enchanted
by black paper shapes blu-tacced to the wall.
Let his happy monosyllables bless us all,
it's still a while until he tests the vanity
of a newly minted tooth against
the rude geometry of a wooden block.
Let us keep our minds away from the skies until then.

Open Heart Surgery

I cut a small sliver of my heart for you.
I remember taking my heart out and holding it,
hot and still beating, in my hand.

I didn't want to slice off too much,
just enough so that the damaged tissue
could regenerate,

but I didn't want to be stingy,
so I tried to get it right on the button,
at the very border of life and death.

So, using a potato peeler,
I cut some slivers from the surface and put the rest,
injured but not terminal, back into my chest.

You asked me what you should do with these slices of heart,
they reminded you
of a doner kebab.

I asked you to appreciate the gesture,
I had gone to such extreme lengths to show you my feelings.
You said a card would have been fine.

I remember how shocked you were
when I phoned a week later and asked
when were you going to give me a slice of your heart.

You said you weren't really ready to get
that serious with anyone and perhaps
we should stop seeing each other.

My heart pulsed coldly

like a war wound the last time
I paid a visit to a kebab shop.

As the hairy armed owner
carved the hot fatty strips of lamb
I glimpsed you through the window.

I wiped the steam away
and saw him holding your hand
your new beloved.

You looked so content,
your smile so wide and breathless,
the first few buttons of your blouse

were shamelessly undone
revealing the new stitches just above your left breast
for all that would dare to look.

Twelve Seconds

I know for a fact that one
of the married guys at my job
pulls into a quiet lay-by
on a B road on his journey home,
takes out his favourite magazine
and beats off for a few minutes.
Then he drives home to his wife,
he eats his dinner and puts the kids to bed.

On my way to the job, I catch
the 0552 from Herne Hill to Victoria.
I board the second last carriage and
nine times out of ten, it's empty.

Now, before you even go there,
I don't do what the married guy does,
I'm single, I can do that whenever,
I do something much worse;
I read a book of poetry,
feet on the opposite seat, 50mph,
I watch Brixton, Battersea power station
and a stretch of the Thames sweep by.
Sometimes I write a few lines of my own.
It's the combination of all these things
that make me feel like a free man,
that I'm somehow malleable, suspended
above my own life's carriage for a moment.

It reached a peak today,
my private carriage crossed the Thames
at sunrise. The water was the same magenta
as a kitchen in my favourite Matisse.

The sun was a huge oriental pastiche of itself
framed by purple curtains of cloud.
This was only visible for the twelve seconds
it took for the train to cross the river
but the big red ghost of that sun
stayed in my mind all day,
and while it remained, no shitty job,
bigoted comment or psychotic boss
could touch me.

I wonder if the image of the lady
in the magazine stays in my workmate's head
before he parks up outside his house.
Does it keep him calm in the traffic?
Does it keep him from throwing
his dinner at the wall?
I only ask this because I don't write
through a belief that I can stop wars
or coax gullible women into my chamber.
If I didn't do this I'd probably end up
killing myself or someone else.
That's why I don't judge the guy in the lay-by.
Art is a fickle label.
We're doing the same thing.

Poem for All the Old Guys that Still Have Elvis Haircuts

I saw one of them getting off the number 3
outside Brixton Town Hall this morning.
He must've been in the last five years of his working life,
but he still had a full head of hair
and he wasn't afraid to use it.

Same cut he must've had since way back
when his best mate slid hot black vinyl from a crisp white sleeve,
snarling You ain't heard nothing yet!
with a newfound curl to his lip.
Then there would be the hard blip
of the needle hitting the groove,
and what happened next was enough
to send our boy home to plunge his fingers
into a tub of Brylcreem and baptise himself.

He'd keep on doing it
through strike and recession,
flower power and moon landings,
even as hair sprouted from his ears
and his abdomen echoed the Vegas years,
he kept on doing it because nothing else
had hit him so hard, searing his soul
and leaving him all shook up uh-huh-huh.

Look out for them, they're everywhere,
standing out from all the other fickle generations
like a well pronounced ring in an oak tree's trunk
signifying that in that particular year
conditions were suddenly extreme and unpredictable.

A Once-Famous Ventriloquist Learns to Cope with the Drudgery of a Normal Life

He still scrapes the odd buck
from his most famous creation,
university shows with the odd f-word
to acknowledge his audience have matured.
Halfwit the Hippo and Lord Lovelunch
didn't kick up a storm on e-bay.

His new voices are slightly skewed
variations of the same theme:
a confident chirp for the bank manager,
a geezerish growl down the pub,
and of course, the stage voice
whenever he's recognised at B&Q.

He cleans a few windows to get by,
mostly for *friends of friends*
catches his weary reflection
as he swipes away the suds,
tries to think of it as another puppet
brilliantly operated by a subtle mind.

Come evening, he dozes
in front of the flicker of his old stage,
the ache of his muscles the symptom
of a new *self* he's building
like the meal ticket he once fashioned
in his father's cluttered shed.

Goodnight my love, he whispers
as he kills the bedside lamp.
Goodnight my darling, I'm so proud of you!
replies the photograph of his ex-wife
pronouncing the *p* in *proud*
with passion and precision.

by heart, on foot

You don't know London until you've walked it,
half-cut, heart-broken, during strange hours,
through the clamour of the daybreak markets
where scent of meat slab mingles with fresh flowers.
You don't know the river until you've trudged
its banks in pissing rain, sans brolly,
your body's atoms remember the flood
in which they frothed during pre-history.
You'll find no Beatrice in those tunnels
just a Metro pull-out on Cheryl Cole.
On this descent you won't bump into Virgil,
no heathen genius among these lost souls.
To find yourself, you have to first get lost.
The river veers before it finds the coast.

A Glass of Water

I'm told by those more erudite than I
at least one atom in a glass of water
has previously passed through Cromwell's bladder
and if that's true, then no-one can deny
the first cool gulp has once in history
been in the squall when Shelley got pulled under,
that filled his lungs and forced him to surrender
his unwritten to blank eternity.

And yet he speaks through me when I recite
his ode to some old god whose shattered face
stands mute for travellers from antique lands.

I'll speak those words next time I urinate,
though words and atoms flow some other place,
we'll meet again next time I wash my hands.

In Defence of the Decision to have Roger Moore Dress Up as a Clown for the Bomb Disposal Scene in Octopussy

Our heroes often seem like clowns at first—
a twitch or piercing stare, too damn intense.
We cannot comprehend their urgent words:
the truth that first appears in gaudy dress
elicits laughter from the seated plebs,
until the ticking bomb pans into view—
the counter running down its final pips,
(collective colons trumpet toodle-loo!)
and what was once the brunt of ridicule
is now the steady hand, the measured grasp,
our final tie to the corporeal,
as open mouthed, we occupy the cusp
of this whole breath, this ever fleeting now
that tears us from our dreams of tomorrow.

On Looking for a Snow Leopard and not Finding One

We find our plot, a Himalayan stretch,
the beaming white, the rippled scars of grey
and, Guru-still, initiate our watch:
wipe the mind and calibrate the gaze.

The markhor bump and grind their clanging skulls,
It could be Croydon on a Friday night,
the quarry, stark and vulnerable, yet still
no feline death-stalk saunters into sight.

We fend off the erosive pangs of doubt
try not to dwell on thoughts of wives and friends,
as vultures watch for where the death-seeds sprout
and film stock runs toward its flapping end.

In dreams we smell her breath and hear her purr,
we push our fingers through her matted fur.

For the Master

"Three-dimensional stop-motion model animation created a fantasy world that was so rare. The way the creatures moved encouraged a sense that one was watching a miracle, but when the miracle becomes commonplace, the concept of the miracles ceases to be miraculous."
-Ray Harryhausen

I learned to dream on Bank Holiday Mondays,
when from the tedium of mid-frame shots,
balsa wood heroes, convoluted plots,
and heroines too shallow to entice-
armies of skeletons would be unleashed,
the Kraken would smash great cities to bits,
and though Medusa's glare gave me the shits,
my young imagination was uncaged.

The thick, black matte-lines helped me to believe
that magic could spontaneously fire
from the dull flint of torpid appearance.

The great conjurer, working in his cave,
could alchemize our nightmares and desires
from steel rods, latex, cotton-wool. Patience.

The Father in Law

He came with the missus, part of the package.
He brought his old chair. His wife's ashes.
He sat there all day, never talking,
not to me or his daughter.
Not to admonish the toddlers
when they threw milk at his trousers.
Not a groan when the dog chewed his toes.
He only opened his mouth to shovel in food
which he chewed slowly, miserably.

He was always the last to leave the living room,
I'd pretend to be interested in Newsnight
hoping he'd go to bed before
they showed those arty films.
Never happened, and when I rose
in the early hours to cut my sandwiches
and head off to the thankless job,
he was there, sat still, scantly lit.
That was when I heard the breathing most;
Innocent particles of oxygen
sucked into the darkest place on earth,
then released, corrupted, polluting the air.
Alone with him, I'd shout
obscenities into his face, did terrible
things to his wife's ashes as he looked on.
Of course, the missus wouldn't put him in a home.
I started thinking that come the day he died,
She'd have him stuffed and sat back on that chair.

The only way that I could get my life back
was if I could make him scream, jump, even twitch.

So I bought a gun from a Polish mate at work,
took it home, stood in front of him, took aim.
Shot the old sod's left ear clean off.
Not a scream, not a jolt, not a bead of sweat
just the smell of hot blood, pouring,
not a tear as I pushed the muzzle into his forehead
not a smile to show that finally, he'd won.

I've heard of men in India that sit
unmoved for years, no food or water,
They do so through some peace they've found within,
But that was never the case with him.
It was some old hatred that kept him going,
something terrible that he would never forgive,
a cold rhythm, fierce quiet where his heart once was.

Homo Erectus Catches the Northern Line Home

*"Suitably clothed and with a cap to obscure his low forehead and beetle
brow, he would probably go unnoticed in a crowd today."*
- Richard Leakey and Alan Walker quoted from National Geographic
*"In his eyes was not the expectant reserve of a stranger but that deadly
unknowing I have seen in a lion's blank yellow eyes."*
- Alan Walker, palaeontologist.
*"…I would put money on him not having a blank animal stare. We would
have recognised him as a fellow human being."*
- Leslie Aiello, anthropologist.

It doesn't matter how we got here.
After a day's work, the nagging of tabloids,
on this vicious, thoughtless urge towards *home*,
our thoughts are far from our origins.

All that matters is that you are *here*,
travelling faster than your species ever dreamed
through dark echoing tunnels, over stern iron bridges,
among this gathering of tiredness and apathy.
With a stolen wallet in your jeans,
a baseball cap disguising your brow ridge,
you've not caused much of a stir among humanity's menagerie.

Your tall, strong body, your stare
that some have conjectured to be similar
to a lion peering blankly from the darkness
has been sufficient in fending off muggers and charity workers.
Yet the glares you have already endured
from well dressed suburbanites, pinstripe gents,
has been enough to teach the survival technique
of staring at the floor.

You are playing this, brilliantly, by ear.
Like the best of us, you have no immediate plans.
Among the lower echelons of this fierce, busy society
a noncommittal grunt will get you far.
You may even find a companion, a mate

among this melee of highly strung, flat faced creatures
and tip-toe away into the gene pool's frequencies.

The dying sun flares back at you
from the windows of passing buildings.
The train is coming to a halt,
the doors about to slide open.
You stand as much of a chance as any of us.
One might venture the hard work is already over.
Now remember to swipe your Oyster at the exit barrier.

dycentra

it's not your fault
that your flowers are the colour
and shape of romantic hearts
which split from the bottom
emitting an immaculate white droplet

while others are moved
to cluck and coo
like rabid aunties
I've always thought of you
as the chris de burg
of the plant world

never mind

may your seeds be sifted
into sachets
to be given away with copies
of the mail on sunday

my notion of heartache
will always be this

a bramble snaking
through a dark alleyway
with only thorns to bare
having given its fruits
too freely

hard is the journey

- after li po

smudged glasses of warm stella
three pounds a pint
damp pitas of pungent meat
costing another fiver

I throw my kebab down
stamp it into the ground
raise my fists and stare
wildly about me

black cabs will not cross
this many bridged river
it's at least another hour before
I can climb the night bus's steps

crossing the bridge
I toss my change over the side
imagine the warm sun
rising over my shoulder

hard is the journey
hard is the journey
so many false short cuts
-bollocks, where am I?

as the change breaks
the waters calm   I sing
a drunk song to the clouds
-sail across the oceans!

empty cinema

take a seat   without popcorn or cola
 house lights up   auditorium empty
the movie doesn't start for twenty minutes
 you watch the blank white screen   enthralled
it only looks like this twenty minutes a day
 sometimes it's a black screen   the same
as the doors and walls when the lights are off
 no   maybe it's a slight glowering rectangle
barely existing thanks to the scant green glow
 of the emergency exit signs
            otherwise
it's adventures   twenty four frames per second
 everyone stares   not knowing
what it really is   in the same way
 they stare at all things- *apples   windows   genitals*
ultimately   a blank white screen
 is the hardest damn thing in the world to look at
try it   within seconds your head is throbbing
 with all those water torture pop songs
images of all those old loves that did or didn't
 things you'd say to the boss if you had a pair

it takes another ten minutes to accept
 white screen   framed in black   silence   inhale   exhale
it's funny   you paid to get in here for noise
 CGI   spectacle   explosions   heroes   heroines
only to find you needed the exact opposite

at which point you're rabbit punched
 by the *pearl and dean* jingle   within seconds
a piss weak american beer becomes your sole passion
 enslaves your tongue to your eye

— 82 —

Cafe

COME ON IN,
say sticky plastic yellow letters
in that warm sizzling fat steam vocabulary of
ALL DAY BREAKFAST
PIE AND MASH
HOT AND COLD DRINKS

Come on in to the worker's cafe
where every table is a smoking table
where you can be that 14 1/2 stone
of unshaven, mud-flecked, callous-palmed,
unshaven, hung-over, foulmouthed,
tobacco-stained, unapologetic
masculinity
that this skimmed cappuccino society
wants to castrate and send to a counsellor

Come on in to the last bastion of the page 3 front
where you can eat your beans, break your wind,
then look to your colleague as if you've done
a rare and wonderful thing

Where you can ask for three sugars
without having to repeat yourself
Where you can leave the Daily Sport open
at whatever page you like
(apart from the horoscopes)

Where the toast is loaded with so much butter
you could lubricate a chainsaw with it

Where you can slag off the boss all you want
'cos you know he's up the road
at the Coffee Republic

Come on in
for full English breakfast £2.20
(£3 with tea or coffee)
Super Special Breakfast £3.60
Mega Special Breakfast £4.25
Vegetarian Breakfast
£1.20

Come on in
bring your headache
bring your divorce
bring your beautiful gut
bring your five day beard
bring your eyes red with whiskey and held back tears
bring your near-relegation second division hopes
bring your pawnshop refuse dreams…

Come on in
take a seat
you don't even have to wipe your feet
'cos hygiene ain't your main concern, yeah we know
that's why we stopped buying soap for the bogs
about a decade ago

That hotplate's gonna keep on sizzling for you
'til half past eight this evening
for breakfast lunch and dinner
that's all the time you need to fill that cantankerous void
'til it's time for the pubs to take over

Acknowledgments

There have been too many helpful souls that have enriched my life, guided my way or put in a good word in the many years since my last publication. A list of names, no matter how long, will always leave someone out. Many thanks to all of you, especially those of you that I have not thanked enough.

*

Gordale Scar was commissioned via the Poetry Society for Tate Etc.
A 1956 Edition of Moby Dick recalls its many years at Clapham Library was commissioned via Apples and Snakes for the opening of the new Clapham Library and its first reading was loudly talked over by a few hundred tipsy architects on the night. It has bobbed about on Soundcloud for about a decade or so before washing ashore in the pages of this book.